Parents need Help Too!

A guide for parents of school-age children

Dr. Tyrone Tanner

ALL RIGHTS RESERVED. No part of this book may be reproduced or transmitted in any form or by any means without written permission from the author.

ISBN (978-0-9834914-0-8)

Educational Concepts, LLC
12320 Barker Cypress Road
Suite 600-111
Cypress, TX 77429
educationalconceptsjournal@gmail.com
Fax: (713) 856-5944

Cover and Interior Layout by Inspired Graphic Designs
(www.inspiredartsanddesigns.com)

First Edition
First Printing April 2011

Library of Congress Cataloging-in-Publication Data
Tanner, Tyrone
Parents Need Help Too: A guide for parents of school-age children/Dr. Tyrone Tanner.
Includes bibliographical references and index.
ISBN 978-0-9834914-0-8
1. Parenting 2. Child Development 3. Balance 4. Education
TX 7-394-219

(Parents Need Help Too: A Guide for Parents of School-Age Children)
Copyright © 2011 by Tyrone Tanner, Educational Concepts, LLC

Ordering Information:

Quantity Sales: Special discounts are available on quantities purchased by corporations, associations, school districts, and others.

Individual Sales: Educational Concepts publications can be ordered directly from the publisher or from most bookstores.

Orders for College Textbook/Course Adoption Use: Please contact Educational Concepts, LLC directly.

For more information on scheduling presentations or other products by Dr. Tanner, please visit:
www.drtyronetanner.com

Available in Spanish

dedication

I dedicate this book to my beautiful daughters, Chelsea and Alana. You continue to inspire me. Your love is the source of my perseverance and makes being a daddy an unbelievable joy.

"Developing a healthy child is easier than repairing a damaged adult."
-Author Unknown

"Creating a healthy family, community, and nation starts with developing healthy children."

-Tyrone Tanner, Ed.D.

table of contents

Introduction 1

Chapter 1 – Child Development and Your Role as the Parent 3

    Parenting Toddlers to Age Six 3

    Seven Years Old to Early Teens 5

    Early Teens to Young Adults 7

Chapter 2- Balance: The Dynamic Force of the School, Parent, and Community 9

Chapter 3- Parenting Through Difficult Times 21

    Parenting As a Single Parent 21

    Parenting Through Divorce 24

    Parenting as the Non-Custodial Parent 28

    Mommy, I Want My Daddy! 29

Chapter 4- Preparing Children for High Stakes Testing 33

    Test-Taking Tips 34

    Common Mistakes 37

    Preparing Children with Learning Disabilities 42

Chapter 5- Voices of Parents: Preparing an Academically Successful Child 45

    Emergent Themes 46

    Networks Versus One-on-One Accountability 52

    Self-Esteem Versus Transmission of Cultural Values 53

    Focus on the Home Environment.. 54

Conclusions and Recommendations 57

References 63

Appendices - Resources for Parents and Schools 67

    Appendix A – Summary of Parenting Strategies 68

    Appendix B - Parent Positive Reinforcement Form 71

    Appendix C - Co-Parenting Agenda Meeting Form 72

    Appendix D - Home Rules Contract 73

About the Author 75

introduction

WHO'S RAISING WHOM? Have you ever noticed a baby crying or a teenager pouting to get his way? From a distance it often sounds the same. I've watched thousands of children over the years raise their parents without the parents noticing they are being controlled or manipulated by their kids. It starts early, as the beautiful baby or toddler wants to be picked up on demand or refuses to sleep in his or her own bed. The cry can be heard from room to room. The parents ask, *What's going on? Why are you crying? Your diaper has been changed and I just fed you. You were fine when I laid you down.* There are countless examples one can use here; just think of one that fits you.

Interestingly enough, as the child progresses, I often see the bewilderment of parents when the child is 16 years old, slamming her door in anger as her mother reads her text messages, views her cell phone log, or reads her e-mail. Once again, I can hear the voices of thousands of parents asking themselves, *What's wrong* or *Where did we go wrong?* Here's the short version. It started years ago, in the infant stages of both the parent's and the child's development.

Whether we are willing to admit it or not, parents usually develop their views on how to parent through some incomplete area within their own being. In other words, parenting is often about our own incompleteness, or areas for which we have failed to gain resolution, stemming from our own childhood. Take, for example, the father who is not active in his child's life because his father was not active in his life. On the other hand, you have the mother, who grew up resenting the strictness of her parents, and now decides to build her relationship around friendship with her child at the sacrifice of raising a child who respects boundaries. While craving affirmation from his own father, the father who grew up seldom seeing or hearing a man express love or affection, now struggles with verbally expressing love to his own children. The point here is that people carry and pass on the impact of areas for which they have failed to gain resolution. I strongly recommend that parents speak with a good life coach or counselor, as we are often blind to many of these areas. Trust me, "developing a healthy child is much easier than repairing a damaged adult" (*Author Unknown*). If we fail to address our own childhood issues, we will undoubtedly pass them on to our children and the cycle will continue from one generation to the next. This book is about developing healthy, balanced parents and children.

chapter one
child development and your role as the parent

Parenting Toddlers Through Age Six

When children are toddlers up to approximately age six, they soak up everything their parents say. They believe what you tell them. Hence, Santa Claus, the tooth fairy, and the Easter bunny are real. Why? Because someone important in their life said it was true. While all stages of development are important, this stage is the time when you can make a huge deposit to their self-esteem. Remind them of how smart and beautiful they are daily, and that beauty is on both the inside and the outside. Recognize them for the small heart-driven moments, such as sharing their toys or snacks with a friend.

As a child, I recall my mother making me feel as though I could leap tall buildings in a single bound. I would draw a stick man and she made me feel as though I was an artist. While I'm clear as an adult that I am far from being an artist, it raised my self-esteem, and eventually I was accepted into a competitive gifted and talented program for art. As a man, or a child in this case, thinks, so he becomes. When I began reading, my mother told everyone how proud she was of her child. I could not wait to read the next book. Later, we would go to the library and read together. Consequently, all of my mother's children are avid readers. As you will later learn, a healthy self-esteem is critical to the healthy development of children.

Discipline is often a word that carries a negative connotation. However, its purpose is to train or teach us to understand the consequences of our actions and their impact on ourselves and others. Discipline could include the rules that you have as parents, rules for games, or rules for a classroom. In any case, children must be taught the appropriate way to behave in different situations. Inappropriate behavior should be corrected using redirection, positive reinforcement, and consequences. For example, when using time-out as a consequence, psychologists recommend one minute for every year of the child's age. This means, if the child is six years old, he or she would be in time-out for six minutes. It should be clear that during this time-out period, you want him or her to think about what the appropriate behavior should have been. Years ago, I learned a modified version of time-out from a creative teacher who had the child draw a picture of the appropriate behavior (positive reinforcement). Educators have long practiced the art of teaching to several modalities or learning styles in children, as this method increases retention. This time-out exercise, forces the child to draw (kinesthetic) a picture of the positive behavior that should have been exhibited (positive reinforcement). This powerful tool also provides a visual for the child. When the child finishes the picture, he or she should be able to explain (verbal and auditory) the appropriate behavior in the picture he or she creatively drew. A sample template is included in the back of this book (Appendix B).

Seven Years Old Through the Early Teens

During the ages of seven to the early teens (11-13), children are becoming impressionable. They no longer just believe what you tell them. They often question you. Yes, you may find yourself asking, *What happened to my sweet baby?* Many directives may be responded to with *"why?"*. Don't be concerned. This is natural and actually beneficial in developing a child's higher order thinking skills, the skills needed to problem solve. During this period, children need to know what we believe and why. I recommend parents have a clear vision and mission of what their core beliefs and values are. Children during this period are ready for a deeper understanding, but need lots of parenting, as they are too old to be babies and too young to be adults. I recommend giving them as much rope as they can handle, but be sure to establish clear boundaries. The goal here is to develop their independence and sense of responsibility.

If you know and are comfortable with the parents of a child in the community, you may allow your child to play next door for a little while. I do not recommend allowing your children to visit the home of another child without knowing both the child and the parents. During this stage, if my child requests to play with her neighborhood friend, I may grant her time to visit to play next door for 30-45 minutes (clear boundaries). Of course, this comes with the permission from the neighboring parent. If my child adheres to the timeline, he or she would be complimented (positive reinforcement) upon returning on time. If he or she does not adhere to the timeline, I would calmly state, *"I'm disappointed Chelsea. You did not adhere to our agreement, as I know you are capable of doing. Unfortunately, you will not be able to go back* (for some designated period of time)." She replies, *"I didn't have my watch."* I respond, *"Whose responsibility was it take your watch?"* She says, with a sad face, *"Mine."* I ask her, *"What could you have done, since you forgot your watch?"* She thinks for several minutes and says, *"I could have had Devon's mother or father tell me when 30 minutes is up, because my daddy said I could only visit for 30-45 minutes."*

This intentional parenting strategy is teaching and developing a critical life skill in the area of responsibility and independence. Your child needs to show you that he or she has earned your trust in order for you to give him or her more rope in this area. During this stage the parent is still using positive reinforcements, redirection, and consequences. However, you are giving them more freedom to develop their own sense of responsibility.

While sad, it is true that one of the variables researchers use to forecast the number of prisons they need to build are third grade test scores. I've dedicated Chapter Three to developing academically successful children. The strongest predictor of incarceration is academic failure in school. If your child is struggling, start early getting him or her the academic support needed.

Early Teens Through Young Adults

During the early teens to young adult years, parents should become more like a coach in their child's life, while never forgetting they are still the parent. This period is often the most challenging period for both the parent and the child. As parents, you cannot force-feed them. There is a delicate balance between encouraging them and challenging their sense of reasoning. I've seen countless failed attempts by parents to force-feed young adults. It usually doesn't work. The parents who have been most successful have challenged their children's thoughts and values. Be patient and remember they are not babies. In fact, they are just a few years away from being considered adults. The problem is that they are not adults and have not had the experiences that adults have had to learn from. Of course, you can't tell them that, as they think they know more than you in their short 16 years of life.

Nonetheless, this is where your years of experience can really serve you as a parent. Be patient. In most cases, we were just like them during this age. We just don't remember. Frequent and daily dialogue is critical. There are certain periods in the education and parenting pipeline where we lose many of our children. Ninth grade is one of those critical periods. Children are usually coming from a smaller middle school to a larger high school with new kids from multiple middle schools. Hormones are active and some parents describe their children as being out of control. I cannot tell you the number of parents, who have contacted me requesting assistance because of some inappropriate text message, phone picture, girlfriend, boyfriend, or computer usage. As a former high and middle school administrator, I've seen quite a bit.

Appealing to the teenager's sense of reasoning is the most effective long-term discipline approach. While I still believe in the same discipline management plan of positive reinforcement, redirection, and consequences during these years, you become a great coach if you are able to help your child see what's best for them. Contracts are effective consequences (templates are available at the end of the book -see Appendix D) as are removing the computer or cell phone if they have one, or restricting their access to important dances or school functions. The key will depend on how good a coach you are and, of course, your teenager. Remind them that you love them, and you know they do not always agree with the decisions you make, but one day they too will be adults and will have to make decisions for their children. When possible, give them options, because it provides them with a sense of control. See Chapter 2 for research-based practices of working with a teenager.

chapter two

Balance: The Dynamic Force of the School, Parent, and Community

Is *loving* a child more important than *raising* a child? Is *teaching* a child more important than the child's *environment* or *physical health*? Which is most important and what happens if we do one more than the other? These questions lead many educators and researchers to ponder: What do children need? There has been an increasing focus on empirically validating academic programs in order to meaningfully answer the question: What works best for children?

All of the questions can be answered with one word: balance. Children need balance. Historically and currently, the main criterion for assessing school readiness has been age (Crnic & Lamberty, 1994). In other words, when a child turns five years old, he or she is typically deemed "ready' for kindergarten. Traditionally, school readiness has been viewed within a maturationist frame, based on chronological criteria, which led to the emergence of readiness testing (Snow, 2006). However, various other approaches have also come to light that address true school readiness in a more balanced way.

When schools and families work cooperatively, they are able to contribute to establishing optimal environments in which children are able to thrive. As such, schools that encourage parents as partners and engage them in decision-making processes that are mutually respectful, realize higher levels of student achievement and greater public support (Muscott, Szczesiul, Berk, Staub, Hoover, & Perry-Chisholm, 2008). The Southwest Educational Development Laboratory also noted that when families, schools, and communities work collaboratively, specific outcomes have been documented, such as higher student achievement; improved student behavior; increased student attendance; and more positive school climates (Henderson & Mapp, 2002). There is no question that establishing effective parent-school partnerships is in the best interest of children and philosophies that will facilitate these partnerships are needed.

The model we will discuss is called PIPES. This is an acronym for physical, intellectual, psychological, environmental, and social growth. PIPES represents a balanced approach to addressing the growth needs of the whole child. This approach is meaningfully different from the traditional view of school readiness in that PIPES is a balanced philosophical approach parents and educators alike can embrace in growing healthy children who thrive in school and in life. Every domain of learning and growing is addressed in the PIPES model. A colleague and I developed this model and have been presenting it across the country for the last several years (McLeod, 2009).

The PIPES philosophy supports building home-school partnerships by implementing a balanced approach to addressing each domain of a child's development. The first domain is physical development. As the body houses the mind, it is of critical importance that children are physically healthy. Lewitt and Baker (1995) reported that more than 75% of teachers indicate that being physically healthy, rested, and well-nourished is an essential aspect of school readiness. Physical well-being and motor development were also included as key factors in the Carnegie Task Force report (1994) on school readiness, as well as being identified as important for students by the National Association for the Education of Young Children (1997). Parents and schools can work collaboratively to contribute to the healthy physical development of the child. The parent-school partnership has the capacity to nurture the physical health of the child through positive exchanges that communicate home routines, positive nutrition habits at school and home, monitoring of the need for hearing and vision checks, updated immunizations, physical activity, and observing and discussing any noticeable physical changes.

Although, the physical domain seems easy enough to maintain, it is one of the most vital. Without giving proper attention to this domain, children may come to school without the necessary stamina to concentrate, listen, focus, retain, participate, apply or make meaningful connections to concepts and principles delivered in the classroom. It is critical that schools and parents work together to be cognizant of the significant changes in the physical development of children in order to contribute to building a balanced and optimal environment in which a child is able to learn and develop. Physical health is affected by many factors, and while the psychological component will be discussed later, it should be noted that there is a direct connection between physical and psychological well-being. When a person does not emotionally and psychologically feel healthy, or is not at peace with life, this disconnect may significantly affect physical health in a variety of ways.

The second component of the PIPES balanced approach is intellectual development. The intellectual component addresses the cognitive or brain-processing development of the child. Although school systems have an established approach to supporting the cognitive development of the child, based on national and local objectives, both the school and the parent must also take into consideration the individual needs of each child.

Children learn best when they are able to attach some meaning to what they are learning. Parents are pioneers in this process. In many schools and homes, communication between adults and children has been ineffective. Unfortunately, on many campuses, teachers and administrators "still think of themselves as individual leaders of classrooms, schools, or districts with little attention to the importance of teamwork and collaboration with parents and community partners" (Epstein & Sanders, 2006).

Likewise, many parents rationalize their reasons as to why they are not able to commit to being involved with the school. Regardless of who shoulders the blame between parents and the school, it is the child who shoulders the consequences.

If optimal conditions for learning are to occur, parents and schools must partner in the process. As noted by the National Association of State Mental Health Program Directors and the National Association of State Directors of Special Education (2002):

"Successful interagency partnerships make every effort to include family members in the decisions and actions that affect their own children. Parents and family members are the experts on their own children, and insofar as possible, they must be allowed, encouraged and supported to participate actively in every aspect of decision making regarding their families' children" (p. 25).

Even so, schools are able to stimulate the intellectual development of students in the absence of parent support; they are simply able to do it better with parenting partnerships.

The third component of the PIPES balanced approach is psychological development. Psychological development can be the most influencing factor of all the domains of the PIPES balanced approach. The psychological approach focuses on intrapersonal development. How children feel about themselves is just as critical as how they think others feel about them. Social and emotional factors directly affect a child's motivation to participate in their environment. Self-conscience must guide the child to cope successfully in current social situations without fear and to perceive themselves as an individual and as member of a group (Sassu, 2007).

McLellan and Katz (2001) compiled a *social attributes checklist* to use as a guideline to a child's social competence. They suggested social competence may be categorized into individual attributes, social skills and peer relationships. Examples used to describe individual attributes characterize children as usually in a positive mood and not excessively dependent on adults. They come to lessons willingly, cope adequately with rebuffs, have the capacity to empathize, have one or two positive relationships with peers already, display a capacity for humor and do not seem to be lonely.

Children who have social competence usually approach others positively, are able to give clear reasons for their actions, assert themselves appropriately, are not easily intimidated by bullies, can enter a group successfully, are able to express frustration and anger without escalating disagreements or harming others, can enter discussions, take turns, show interest in others, negotiate compromises appropriately, do not draw inappropriate attention to self, and accept and enjoy peers and adults from other ethnic groups. Peer relationship examples depict children as usually accepted by others, sometimes invited by others to play and work, and being named by other children friends.

The fourth component of the PIPES balanced approach is the environmental domain. The environmental domain addresses how the home and school environment influences a child's development. Conditions under which children function in their environment may contribute to their healthy development or take away from developmental progression. Schools are just as responsible as parents for providing an environment for children to thrive in. Schools that have poor lighting, landscaping, flooring, walls, and are generally not kept up are sending a subliminal message that says, "We don't care." One of the mandates of effective schools research suggests that effective schools have a safe and orderly environment. Schools, just as homes, will have occasional maintenance breakdowns. How long they stay inoperable is what influences the environment that would be more effective for a child to thrive in. According to the Learning First Alliance (2010), students are more likely to thrive academically – as well as socially and emotionally – in schools they experience as safe and supportive. A synthesis of the research suggested four elements are essential to creating and maintaining safe and supportive places of learning:

1. Support: A supportive learning community, including challenging curriculum, respectful relationships, and student participation and leadership.

2. Systems: Systematic approaches to supporting safety and positive behavior, including school-wide approaches, orderly classrooms and a continuum of supports for students in need.
3. Collaboration: Involvement of family, students, school staff and the community.
4. Standards: Standards and measures to support continuous improvement based on data.

The physical safety and health of the environment that a child thrives in greatly influences the capacity in which a child is able to engage in the environment and use the environmental attributes to develop in a healthy way.

The fifth component of the PIPES balanced approach is social development. The social domain specifically addresses a child's interpersonal development. Transitions in school structure and peer network dynamics provoke distress even in the absence of negative social experiences (Erath, Flanagan, & Bierman, 2007). The influence of peers and social groups has been an undeniable force that influences the interpersonal and intrapersonal development of a child. Friendships become particularly important as youth enter adolescence, where they experience strong desires for personal validation through interpersonal intimacy (Parker, Rubin, Erath, Wojslawowicz, & Buskirk, 2006). The school and the home can contribute to the healthy development of a child throughout life; however, early adolescent and adolescent development can significantly shape how they are able to maintain adult social relationships. The skills needed to maintain conversations, such as sensitive verbal responses, may become particularly important for establishing and maintaining friendships during the early adolescent years, when friendships increasingly involve reciprocated self-disclosure and intimacy (Parker et al., 2006). These skills require a high level of self and social regulation, including the capacity to sustain interpersonal attention, regulate negative affect, and maintain positive interpersonal interest and orientation (Erath et al., 2007). In short, children need to be taught the proper manners for dealing with certain situations.

The philosophy of the PIPES balanced approach suggests that all of the domains are of critical importance. Through the supportive contributions of parents and schools, the PIPES can be implemented in the lives of children. Successfully addressing the needs of students in the public school system requires that stakeholders address the child holistically, keeping balance with all of the factors. When they are haphazardly introduced or are unbalanced, the results are readily apparent. For example, the focus of schools is on the intellectual development. However, without taking into consideration the other dimensions of child development, schools graduate students who later *flunk* in life. As it is now, schools on the K-16 pipeline are doing a marginal job, at best, in graduating students.

Research supports that youth will respond to the rigor of an educational curriculum if teacher-student partnerships and nurturing relationships are created that seek to understand students holistically (Charles & O'Quinn, 2001). An academic focus is important, however, in high poverty schools and schools with a preponderance of diverse learners (children with different learning styles). Student success is more readily encountered when the academic focus is delivered through relationships founded on a principle of trust (Ogbu, 2003; Foster, 2005). In delivering equitable academic opportunities for all students, stakeholders must become activists in advocating for the rights of their students by building classroom environments that create independent cultures or cultures that lead to both student and teacher success. In building these cultural environments, teachers and parents, like their students, should implement the PIPES philosophy in their personal lives as well as support the development of the PIPES balanced approach in the lives of their students.

Student potential becomes limitless when a teacher has the competence, confidence and the courage to step beyond traditions and do what is necessary for student mastery and evidential success (Carter, 2004). Transitioning to a PIPES philosophy is going beyond the family or the teacher's individual values, experiences, resources and understandings to embracing the collective strengths students contribute to the overall environment through healthy relationships that balance their quality of life. Schools and parenting partnerships can make a difference. In fact, they have been making a difference. It is that difference that determines the stance of the nation's students. Are the stakeholders in the lives of public school children positioning students for equitable life opportunities, or are they contributing to social inequality? In this time of challenge, external and internal stakeholders can choose to control for academic deficits and inequalities, but more importantly, they have the power to eliminate them.

chapter three
Parenting Through Difficult Times

Parenting as a Single Parent

Raising a child or children is clearly a two-parent job. It is the hardest and most important job a parent will have in life. When one parent is solely raising a child, the word *tough* is an understatement. Yet this situation is the reality of many homes.

> *Only 29% of children under the age of three live with two parents,* meaning **71% do not.**

If you are a single parent, meaning the non-custodial parent is not involved or is involved very little, you will have to be well organized, as parenting, at the minimum, clearly requires the efforts of two.

It is hard for couples to understand the loneliness and fears that come from solely having to do it all. My heart goes out to you.

I recommend first finding a little time for yourself, as you cannot afford to break down. You are all that your child has. This act is important; it means you will need to strategically build support systems that include other parents who can give you the moments you need to stay healthy. Tap into friendships and family, as you will need a support system. Resist the notion or guilt that you need to do it all. It has been said, *It takes a village to raise a child.* That village is even more important for single parents.

Maintain your physical health. It is not only good for your physical well-being, but it impacts your psychological well-being. Most gyms have a child care center, and if not, get a stroller and walk the neighborhood. If the child is older, walk or jog together. It's an excellent bonding experience while simultaneously teaching the importance of taking care of oneself.

Speaking of psychological benefits, remind yourself daily that you are fortunate. There are always individuals in a much worse position. In other words, if you have a negative view, I'm charging you to change that view to look for the positives in your life. Our minds are interesting; they will always find the evidence to support our views. If you tell yourself your skin is horrible, your mind will help your eyes find every blemish on your body. As another example, have you ever purchased a new car and noticed that all of a sudden everywhere you go someone is now driving your same make and model? If you call the car dealership and ask them about the production, they will tell you production or sales did not significantly go up this week. The only change is that your mind is now looking or focusing on the make and model of your new car. Single parents, focus on the good in your life. If you are reading this book, you have taken the first step in improving your relationship with your children.

As a single parent, organization is paramount. A large academic calendar is a must. Write the major school events, activities, or appointments on this calendar. The large calendar is great because it allows you to see what you have to do for the entire year. Lastly, choose healthy relationships. As a single parent, there is no room in your life for unhealthy relationships. This may even include limiting the time you spend with family members. If they are negative or unhealthy, you have to protect both yourself and the well being of your child. When you are ready to start dating, or if you are already dating, make sure the individual is someone whose major views regarding raising children line up with yours. If he or she is going to take you, they need to understand that it's a package. I'm a firm believer that you need to have these basic questions comfortably addressed before introducing someone new into the life of your child.

If you have made mistakes, forgive yourself; you are not perfect. Take care of yourself (PIPES), as you will not be any good to anyone, including your child, if you fall apart. Develop healthy and dependable support systems, get organized, and surround yourself with healthy relationships.

Parenting Through Divorce

The single greatest determinant of a child's adjustment to separation or divorce is the ability of the parents to co-parent. It is easy for parents to forget the emotional effects that children experience from separation or divorce. Feelings often include depression, guilt, denial, and fear. It truly is an adjustment period for everyone.

Children need to hear and know that they did not cause the separation or divorce and that they will be taken care of, as the changes often bring insecurities.

They wonder why the other parent is not a part of their life. Even if the parent was never actively involved, children will question their whereabouts. Reinforce to the child, or children, that both parents love them. In the midst of divorce this may be difficult, as each parent is going through their own life adjustment, but give the child permission to love both parents. Children need to positively identify with both of their parents.

When children have to split their loyalty between two people they love, it often results in confusion, guilt, and withdrawal.

Children often do not feel comfortable sharing their true feelings with the custodial parent for fear of losing this parent as well. Again, the result is suppressed anger that usually causes serious issues for the child later in life. I've spoken with several adults who are still dealing with the aftermath of parents who were unable to put their differences aside for their children. Depending on the situation, the adult may now demonstrate serious distrust of both women and men, among other issues, which can significantly impact their ability to develop healthy relationships in their adult life. What a travesty to pass this on to our children.

Never make negative remarks about the other parent to the child.

If necessary, find a friend, relative, counselor, or even a dog to confide in, but by no means share your ill feelings with your child. This includes indulging in hostile discussions with the other parent in front of the child. In fact, most literature suggests keeping the child completely out of the divorce. This includes never passing messages through the child to the other parent. Transitions should be peaceful and include moments of happiness. Again, filter every action through the lens of what is in *the best interests of the child.* While going through a divorce is difficult for everyone, it is recommended that parents allow children to express their feelings because it becomes an outlet as well as a means of gauging how the child is handling the separation.

> ***Parents should remain patient and aware that the child is going through major adjustments.***

Routines have now changed. Clothes and toys have to be packed and brought back and forth, all the while often adjusting to a different structure, new home, bed, and school. Children may also feel grief for the loss of the absent parent each time the child must separate from either parent.

When dealing with your ex-spouse, determine the best means of communication. You must communicate since you have a child together, and it is in the child's best interest that you communicate with each other. Set a business-like tone with your ex-spouse and be respectful and courteous. Communicate with your ex-spouse as if you were writing or speaking to a colleague; be respectful and cordial. At minimum, you want to always be amicable. This approach is much easier once you have forgiven yourself, as well as your ex-spouse, for the failed marriage. People often mask forgiveness or state they have forgiven, when, in reality, they have only suppressed their hurt and anger. This is a clear sign that forgiveness has not really taken place. On a side note, forgiving actually releases the forgiver to move on with their life.

When communicating with your spouse, make requests, not demands. Again, when you are angry, it is hard to be nice. Even if you fake niceness, your ex will pick up whether you are being genuine. Try to meet and talk consistently. My ex and I usually call to tell our daughter goodnight when she is with the other parent or not with us. It allows the parent not in possession to have a brief moment with their child. It also helps the child see that while mommy and daddy do not live together they are friends. Friends may be a far stretch, but in their minds it translates, therefore it is okay to show love to the other parent in front of the parent in possession. This is important, because part of the confusion for children, often stemming from the divorce, is where do I place my loyalty?

Always keep the conversation centered on the kids. If your ex-spouse deviates, refocus the conversation back to the child. To the degree possible, always communicate from the perspective of the child's best interest (see the co-parenting form in the back of this book). The key to mastering this goal is separating emotion from behavior, which is significantly helped when you have forgiven your ex-spouse.

Because you are dealing with people's feelings and emotions, listen to their heart. Your goal is to improve the relationship with your ex-spouse for the sake of your children. It takes emotional maturity and work. Ask them their opinions. This shows you value their input, as you should. Give them credit for the good they do with and for your child. It is not a competition.

You must work together, you divorced each other not your children. A developmentally healthy child will take input from both of you. Lastly, recognize that you will have to release the small stuff. If your ex-spouse does things you do not agree with that are not detrimental, let it go. Your child, with love from both parents working together, will be fine. Children are resilient. They need love more than your control, guidance more than your friendship, and your presence more than presents.

Parenting as the Non-Custodial Parent

As the non-custodial parent, you feel a loss of control. You may grieve not having your children as much as you were accustomed. It may appear you have less influence, and you may even feel guilty about moving on with or even enjoying your life. Let me be clear, with the exception of grieving for more time with your children, none of the above is true. In most cases, you still have a lot of control and influence.

Most states will grant joint managing conservatorship as a rule. This means you are entitled to your children's medical, school, and other records. You have the right to make appointments with school officials and request that information be sent to both parents. You can be involved as much as you choose. With younger children, I recommend having lunch with your child as often as possible. They enjoy it. Call them and mail them letters, often. Young children love going to the mailbox and getting a letter. A five-minute note makes their day.

You will have to learn your rights, which are usually the same, with the exception of the right to determine residence. I recommend the non-custodial parent request a geographical restriction that prevents the ex-spouse from moving to a location far from the area where the two of you live. It is in the best interest of children to have frequent contact with both parents as much as possible. If one parent moves far way and prevents or reduces frequent contact, it is usually not in the child's best interest. Understand your legal rights and don't take for granted that your ex's interpretation of the law is correct. The interpretation will usually serve his or her interest, not yours, and may not serve the child's.

You will need to take the same approach, mentioned in the Parenting Through Divorce section of this chapter, regarding communication. Communication is the key to co-parenting. Always be respectful and remember it's about the best interest of the child. Resist withdrawing and just starting over, which often happens with many non-custodial parents. Your children need you and you need them. The love of a child is the greatest source of strength. There have been many times in my life that the love of my children strengthened me to fight for both of them, and what I felt was in their best interest.

Mommy, I Want My Daddy!

This section is dedicated to parents who are unclear of how important the roles of both parents are in the healthy development of children. Often fathers do not understand the importance of their role, and mothers don't value the father's role (see the statistics below):

> - *85% of children who are incarcerated come from homes with limited to no father involvement (Fulton County Georgia jail populations, Texas Department of Corrections, 1992).*
> - *85 % of children with psychological issues come from homes with limited to no father involvement (Center for Disease Control).*
> - *72% of dropouts come from homes with limited to no father involvement (National Principals Association Report on the State of High Schools).*
> - *63% of children who commit suicide come from homes with limited to no father involvement (United States D.H.H.S. Bureau of the Census).*

I could go on for hours regarding the statistics supporting the importance of fathers being involved, but I think the point is made. Fathers, your role is important, and don't allow anyone to make you think differently. The research reflects that some mothers often diminish the importance of the children's father in the life of their children.

> *Overall, approximately 50% of mothers "see no value in the father's continued contact with his children...."* (Source: Surviving the Breakup, Joan Kelly & Judith Wallerstein, p. 125)
>
> *In a study: "Visitational Interference - A National Study" by Ms. J Annette Vanini, M.S.W. and Edward Nichols, M.S.W., it was found that 77% of non-custodial fathers are NOT able to "visit" their children, as ordered by the court, as a result of "visitation interference" perpetuated by the custodial parent.*
>
> *89% of mothers see no value in their husband's input when it comes to handling problems with their kids (Source: EDK Associates survey of 500 women for Redbook Magazine. Redbook, November 1994, p. 36)*
>
> *40% of mothers reported that they had interfered with the father's visitation to punish their ex-spouse (Source:Stanford Braver, American Journal of Orthopsychiatry)*

Again, there are a lot of statistics to support these claims, and I'm sure there are several reasons why this happens, but none are important. The issue here is to bring clarity to the fact that the father is vitally important to the upbringing of the children. I often hear mothers say, *If he (referring to the father) does not want to be there, I don't need him. We are just fine.* Another common statement is that the father's parenting style or values are different. The fathers usually stated they are unable to deal with drama and/or the issues surrounding trying to communicate with their ex, so they stop trying. *If she (meaning the mother) does not need me, she can handle it by herself. It is easier for me to just start over.* In the above example, there is a lot of displacement occurring at the sacrifice of the child. The mother needs help, and the father is being a coward by throwing in the towel at the sacrifice of his children.

For mothers who have endured struggles, you must get the necessary healing and respect your child's father for the sake of your children. Fathers, you must be responsible; nothing should come in between spending your time and your resources on your child. The key here is for mothers and fathers to remove self and focus on the best interest of the child.

chapter four
Preparing Children for High Stakes Testing

We live in an age of accountability. Children are being tested almost every year. In fact, state exams often determine if a student moves to the next grade level or even graduates. The accountability is driving the test craze. Everyone faces accountably. At the school level, financial rewards are granted to high-performing schools and low-performing schools are closed or restructured. At the educator level, teachers and principals are often given bonuses for high classroom test scores, and poor performing teachers are removed or replaced as a result of low classroom test scores or campus scores. At the student level, promotion to the next grade level and receiving a diploma all depend on the results of a high-stakes test. Proponents state that high-stakes tests close the achievement gap, while opponents state that the tests do not adequately assess the student's ability. Regardless of your view, high stakes tests are a part of children's lives today, and parents need to do whatever they can to ensure their children are successful.

Test Taking Tips

The following are several test-taking strategies from the article *10 Common Test Mistakes* by Grace Flemming (2010. p.1). Flemming includes several techniques that parents should consider using to help their children with taking high-stakes tests (provided below). I also recommend speaking with your child's teacher, as they may have different techniques that they have been practicing with your child. In this case, reinforcing those strategies at home with your child is very beneficial. It is also important to encourage your child to do their best. While the test is important, it cannot assess all of your child's talents and gifts. Below are several generally recommended test-taking strategies:

1) **Use the process of elimination.** Show your child how to eliminate the answers that are wrong.

2) **Underline important information.** Check your state rules, but usually a child can underline or highlight important information in the reading selections. Parent, you need to spend a lot of time practicing this ahead of time.

3) **Use SQ3R.** A classic reading comprehension strategy, that works well for test taking.

S is for Skim. Teach your child to look for underlined

headings, for words in italics or bold face, and to read the first sentences of paragraphs.

Q is for Question. Model asking questions about the text. What was the selection about? For example, if the selection is about sailing: What makes the sailboat go? Who are famous sailors?

The First R is for Read.

The Second R is for Review: This is a good time to answer your questions.

Third R is for Re-read.

4) Do the Easy Ones First. Teach your child to look through the items that they find easiest first. Be sure they are filling the ovals correctly. This gives them more time to do the more difficult ones.

5) Mask the Test. Show the child how to cover one column with a paper so they are not overwhelmed by the amount of text or so they can focus on the important stuff. You may also cut a window in a paper or file folder so the student can move the mask from question to question. A mask would also work well for students whose eyes wander and need help filling in the correct test bubbles.

6) Eat and drink wisely on the morning or day of the test. Make sure your child doesn't go into the test hungry.

Hunger can interfere with concentration and so can the noise of a rumbling stomach. Don't create an unnecessary and unfortunate distraction!

7) **Don't forget to wear a watch.** Children need to be taught how to pace themselves. This will require them to have a watch in order to keep an eye on the minute hand while they're testing.

8) **Arrive early to the classroom.** Make sure your child has enough time to relax and reflect for several minutes before the test begins.

9) **Look over the entire test as soon as you receive it.** Teach your child to evaluate the test, in order to determine how much time they should spend on each section. For instance, if there is a multiple choice section followed by two large essay questions, remind the child that they must be sure to give themselves enough time for the essays. Assign a time limit to each section. They can always go back if they finish early.

10) **Pay close attention to directions.** Read them twice, if possible. Don't make assumptions.

11) **For multiple choice questions, try to answer the

question before looking at your choices. If you're right, one of the choices will match your answer.

12) Every time you skip a question, be sure to mark it. A common mistake that children make is leaving an answer blank by accident. Ouch--what a waste. Teach your child to make a star beside questions if they skip them. Don't leave any blanks.

13) For defining terms, concentrate on themes and chapter titles. Teach your child the following strategy: If you're facing a list of terms to define and you're unsure about a few, think back to major themes (usually found in chapter titles). Ask yourself: where might that term have appeared? Take a guess if you're not sure. You may get partial credit if you're close.

14) Stay positive! Children must be taught that if they start to doubt themselves, they may go blank. Encourage them to keep concentrating on their strengths.

Common Mistakes

The following errors are the most common mistakes students make when taking a high-stakes test (Flemming, 2010). These errors, and the solutions that accompany them, should be reviewed with your child before they begin the testing process.

1) Leaving an answer blank.

There is nothing wrong with skipping over a tough question to give yourself some extra time to think it over-- just as long as you remember to go back to the question later. The danger is forgetting to go back to every question you've skipped. A blank answer is always a wrong answer!

Solution: Each time you skip a question, put a check mark beside it.

2. Answering a question twice.

You'd be surprised how many times students choose two answers in multiple choices. This makes both answers wrong!

Solution: Review your work and make sure each true/false and multiple-choice question only has one answer circled!

3. Transferring answers incorrectly from scratch paper.

The most frustrating mistake for math students is having an answer correct on the scratch paper, but transferring it wrong to the test!

Solution: Double-check any work you transfer from a scratch sheet.

4. Circling the wrong multiple-choice answer.

This is a costly mistake, but one that is very easy to make. You look over all the multiple choice answers and pick the one that is correct, but you circle the letter next to the correct answer—the one that doesn't match your answer!

Solution: Make sure the letter/answer you indicate is the one you really mean to select.

Cross out the answers you have eliminated as you did the process of elimination.

5. Studying the wrong chapter.

Whenever you have a test coming up, make sure that you understand which chapters or lectures the test will cover. There are times when a teacher will test you on a specific chapter that is never discussed in class. On the other hand, the teacher's lectures may cover three chapters, and the test may cover only one of those chapters. When that happens, you can end up studying material that won't appear on your exam.

Solution: Always ask the teacher which chapters and lectures will be covered on a test.

6. Ignoring the clock.

One of the most common errors students commit when taking an essay test is failing to manage time. This is how you end up in a panic with 5 minutes to go and 5 unanswered questions staring back at you.

Solution: Always take the first few moments of an exam to assess the situation when it comes to essay questions and answers. Give yourself a time schedule and stick to it. Give yourself a set amount of time to outline and answer each essay question and stick to your plan!

7. Not following directions.

If the teacher says "compare" and you "define," you are going to lose points on your answer. There are certain directional words that you should understand and follow when you take a test.

Solution: Know the following directional words:

Define: Provide a definition.
Explain: Provide an answer that gives a complete overview or clear description of the problem and solution for a particular question.
Analyze: Take a part a concept or a process, and explain it step by step.
Contrast: Show differences.
Compare: Show likenesses and differences.
Diagram: Explain and draw a chart or other visual to illustrate your points.
Outline: Provide an explanation with headings and

subheadings.

8. Thinking too much.

It's easy to over-think a question and begin to doubt yourself. If you tend to second-guess yourself, you will inevitably change a right answer to a wrong answer.

Solution: If you are a person who tends to over-think, and you get a strong hunch when you first read an answer, go with it. Limit your thinking time if you know you tend to doubt your first instincts.

9. Technological breakdown.

If your pen runs out of ink and you can't complete an exam, your blank answers are just as wrong as they would have been for any other reason. Running out of ink or breaking your pencil lead halfway through a test sometimes means leaving half your exam blank.

Solution: Always bring extra supplies to an exam.

10. Not putting name on test.

There are times when failing to put your name on a test will result in a failing grade. This can happen when the test administrator doesn't know the students, or when the teacher/administrator won't see students again after the test is over (like at the end of a school year). In these special situations (or even if you have a very stern teacher), a test that doesn't have a name attached to it will be tossed out.

Solution: Always write your name on a test before you get started!

Preparing Children with Learning Disabilities for High-Stakes Testing

Although there are special provisions for students with learning disabilities, parents should still provide support tailored to their student. Below, I provide tips for parents to use in preparing children with learning disabilities to take high-stakes tests.

1) Ensure that your child's Individualized Education Plan (IEP) clearly spells out appropriate accommodations for both testing situations and classroom work. Find out if your child will be permitted to use accommodations for testing that he or she has already been using as part of everyday learning.

2) Find out if there are any accommodations that your child needs that your state, district, or school does not allow.

3) Speak with your child's teacher and IEP team to determine what accommodations your child needs while taking high-stakes tests.

4) Make sure your child has been taught the content. Sometimes students with a learning disability (LD) have not had the adequate instruction time.

chapter five

Voices of Parents: Preparing an Academically Successful Child

In this chapter, we will discuss different factors that directly influence the academic success of students. Understanding and practicing the themes discussed will help you, as a parent, to improve your child's chances for advancement and success in both school and the global marketplace. The information in this chapter is based on a study I conducted of different ethnic groups and their influences on the educational success of their children.

One of the biggest findings of the study was that parents play a major role in creating home environments that are conducive to learning. When a great deal of energy is placed on establishing strong educational foundations for the child, the benefits are evident. It was also noted that communication barriers often limit the time that parents volunteer at their children's schools. Some parents also have time constraints that impact their ability to participate in school functions such as parent-teacher organizations. In the absence of being able to physically partner with the school, there are many things you, as a parent can do to help your child.

In the study, I examined how the parents of academically successful children positively influenced their children's educational values. The themes revealed in the study illustrated that although the children of the parents studied and achieved similar educational outcomes, the processes varied considerably between the groups. The variety of paths traveled to educational success by the groups cautions us against stereotyping students, while it also encourages educational leaders to consider the important role parents play in a child's academic success. Presented below is a brief summary of each theme.

Emergent Themes

Looking at data regarding academic achievement sparked an interest in unearthing the formula behind the success of identified high-achieving students. Variables such as parental income and education, two components of socioeconomic status which traditionally predict individual academic achievement and generally serves to differentiate between ethnic groups, failed to explain the educational outcomes of these high-achieving students. Many of the students in this study came from families with a lower socioeconomic status, but outperformed their counterparts from more privileged backgrounds. An inability to solve the puzzle became the motivating force that drove the present study.

Like most parents do, each brought specific values and beliefs to the table. In this study, parental investment and involvement in their children's lives suggested students do well in school due to the internalization of certain values and traditions such as respecting one's teachers and obeying one's parents. The first theme discovered, *Parental Transmission of Cultural Values*, is characterized by the relationship between the values and norms of the family's culture and the academic success of the children. When parents instill the belief that education is important to success, their offspring are more likely to experience upward mobility.

If cultural identity formation were handed down from high-achieving parents to children equally within various groups, this would imply the irrelevance of race as a distinctively disadvantaging status characteristic. Therefore, if children have similarly shared values, their education attainment would be similar, regardless of their ethnic background. The researcher probed to discover if and when parents attain the same level of schooling, do children perform in school at the same level and progress through school in the same way, or are there other differences resulting from other socioeconomic distinctions?

The *Home Environment* emerged as the second theme. As the label implies, the theme addressed the in-home parental support available to children. This support included parents providing a number of resources such as tutors and books, or whatever else was needed, to assist their children. Resources and networking, coupled with a strong academic foundation, emerged as having the capacity to transform experiences inside and outside the home environment sufficiently to overcome any race-related differences such as language. This piece was found to significantly assist students in their pursuit of academic excellence.

The next theme, *Academic Foundations*, refers to the importance placed on making sure each child had a great start in school. Parents were found to provide emotional support, encouragement and structure for their children in order to help build a sturdy academic foundation as they invested themselves in their children. Parental strategies for academic success shape their children's identities and their peer relations. For example, one key strategy for success included preparing children for the next grade level before they entered the school. This mechanism, through which parents' personal resources, including the resources that came with their more advanced level of schooling, passed through to their children and promoted academic success.

It is also important that parents are aware of the larger picture within which family systems and school are embedded and which allows them to network and then channel their young children along different educational pipelines. To better understand the interaction between the parents' economic situations and students' educational experiences requires awareness of the familial networking. Its influence is crucial in shaping children's friendships and educational activities.

How beliefs are translated into actions related to education and friendships and how students perceive or accept such parental control is equally important. The fourth theme, *Role Modeling*, deals with the modeling of behaviors parents expect of their children. This includes modeling behaviors such as reading and making use of study or resource facilities like the library. The students' personal identities become defined by the attitudes and behaviors that their parents model. During the research, I also discovered that cultural identities, modeled for children at home by their parents and at school by peers, are linked to perceptions of success in school. Interviews revealed the importance of parental and peer congruence for interpretations of acceptable academic behaviors, extra-curricular activities, and choices of friends and careers. The congruence functioned to make the children realize the sacrifices their families made for them. Even without having luxuries such as video games and popular clothes, seeing their parents' willingness to spend their limited financial resources on books and school-related materials, helped the children to realize that their parents hold school and learning in the highest regard.

The parents studied also built strong *Parental and Peer Networks* of persons who knew the policies of schools and who spoke better English to help guide and counsel them through the system. The emergence of this theme, while not accounted for in previously considered theories, is explained in an examination of *Human Capital Theory*. *Human Capital Theory* explains how socioeconomic factors influence parental investment decisions in education, which in turn affect their children's preferences and cognitive skills and thus shape educational success (Rumberger and Larson, 1998). In the present study, although family or ethnic community networks provided a powerful human capital element to aid parents, the mere existence of family networks was not sufficient. What mattered most was the quality and stability of the network relationships. Being connected to this type of *cultural grapevine* supplied the parents with information on how school issues should be addressed. Parents could also make comparisons between their children and their peers' children as they interacted within their networks.

By discussing the expectations of mainstream America, children were better able to respond when their cultural values conflicted with mainstream beliefs. Although parents felt that their children should know their cultural/ethnic history, they were adamant about not dwelling on it. Their children's focus was on the future and the importance of overcoming the odds by valuing education.

To enable their children's success, parents also focused on *Protecting Their Children's Self-Esteem.* This theme functioned to illustrate that parents did not expect the world to support their children or build their self-esteem. Parents themselves felt the need to celebrate the daily accomplishments of their children and to accentuate the positive attributes of their children and their culture. It seemed that the families tended to rely heavily on family and friends in forming an academic identity, rather than taking cues from school personnel and the performance feedback conveyed by grades and achievement test scores.

Another theme that emerged was *Varied Levels of School Participation*. Although parents do not always have the opportunity to volunteer at school functions due to work schedules, they did assure school stakeholders that someone was looking out for their children's well being by having face-to-face meetings with the teachers.

A major theme was *Holding the School and Their Children Accountable,* which was very important to parents. Here it was evident that parents felt a need to be in constant communication with the school and their children as it related to academic success. The parents made it clear to the teachers that they wanted their children to do well in school and to be successful later in life. In an effort to hold their children accountable, the parents insisted upon proof of task completion from their children. These themes, when analyzed together, revealed many insightful corollaries. Therefore, the following section provides a discussion of these themes considered together.

In this case, cultural capital may provide a deeper explanation for parents' value for education. Immigrant parents often come to America believing that education is the key to upward social mobility. This cultural belief, translated into capital, academically aids children. These beliefs defy many socio-economic theories that suggest that socio-economic status positions one towards academic success. In this study, all of the participant parents came to America poor, but they obtained high levels of education and emphasized and modeled the importance of education to their children.

Networks Versus One-on-One Accountability

It should also be noted that although some of the parents in this study demonstrated distrust, they responded to their distrust differently. Some established strong cultural networks or human capital structures that advised them on school policy, whereas others acted out their distrust with a more brash *in your face* approach. While the parents taught their children mainstream values and expectations, they believed it was necessary to show the teachers and the school that their children were not alone and were cared about by having face-to-face conferences and confronting policies that they found to be disagreeable.

As a result of the covert distrust demonstrated by some immigrant parents and cultural respect for authority steeped in the culture, school conflicts seldom occurred for the participants in this study. In the context of this research, it should be noted that many immigrant parents verbalized that they trusted the American system. However, their reliance on network leaders to resolve potential conflicts is exemplary of a passive distrust of sorts. Possibly, as a result of this variable, not passivity, mainstream America has been more accepting of some immigrant parents.

On the other hand, some parents have historically had an arduous struggle for the rights they have obtained throughout their history in America. As a result, they have had no problem with overtly displaying their distrust. For some parents, this historically-developed confrontational spirit was evident with a more direct and overt *in your face* approach to resolving school problems. This theme described situations when parents needed to hold the school accountable by having face-to-face conferences with teachers at the school or by soliciting the assistance of the media to address school concerns not resolved by the one-on-one approaches. Obviously, the manner in which the parents demonstrated and responded to their distrust has had varying effects on the policies, beliefs, and views of parents. According to critical race theory, these different views may contribute to school practices and policies that are not in the best interest of certain minority cultures.

Self-Esteem Versus Transmission of Cultural Values

The researcher discovered that parents were similar in their ultimate motives for academic success, but that they differed in their approaches to increase their children's confidence. Some parents believed that they must increase and safeguard their children's self-esteem at home because the school system and the larger society do not perform an adequate job for minorities. Therefore, an emphasis was placed by the participants in this study on displaying their children's report cards and graded assignments on the walls and on refrigerator doors. They believed it was crucial to teach their children of the accomplishments of similar ethnic inventors who contributed to society as a whole. Although they felt that schools are responsible for teaching this part of history, they also took this responsibility into their homes in order to inspire and protect their children's self-esteem and pride. This distrust of the system is consistent with Ogbu's theory regarding the behaviors of involuntary immigrants, and in this case, it manifests itself by parents filling in the gaps of a school system that fails to meet their expectations.

On the other hand, the parents in my study protected and inspired their children's self-esteem and pride through role modeling; not just role modeling by reading or going to the library, but also by teaching fundamental principles. Traditions and values remain a part of the cultural capital that aids parents in protecting their children's self-esteem.

Focus on the Home Environment

Parents in the study created a home environment conducive to learning. They provided a number of resources routinely. However, many parents felt the in-home resources were necessary due to a lack of sensitivity for diverse learning styles and interests. In essence, many parents stated that they felt a need to assure and increase their children's understanding of the school's curriculum and its expectations. As one parent stated, she provided visuals and interactive videos to help her child understand what was being taught.

Interestingly, all parents strictly monitored the completion of their children's homework assignments, albeit for different reasons. Among some parents, this was part of the theme that dealt specifically with holding the school accountable. They believed that it was necessary to verify school recommendations with outside sources.

Other parents strictly monitored their children's assignments through elementary and middle school and slowly shifted the responsibility onto their children by high school. By the time the children reached high school, the parents ceased actual supervision of homework and only asked their children if they had finished their homework.

Interestingly, minority parents demonstrated a stricter level of monitoring that continued throughout high school. By stricter, the research points to a requirement by the parents in this study for their children to show them each completed homework assignments. In essence, the parents wanted to verify that the work was truly completed.

I shared the research from my study to undergird the suggestions and recommendations for cultivating and producing socially and academically well-rounded children provided here in this chapter and throughout the book. One commonly espoused philosophy is *knowledge is power*. This statement is so true, and when we apply knowledge of best practices to support children, their parents, society and *the kids* (most importantly) benefit.

Conclusions and Recommendations

The findings of the research and work in schools suggest that successful parenting strategies strongly influence children's ultimate academic success. As the community stakeholders, the parents' reduced school participation due to hectic work schedules, language, or other cultural constraints, did not signal a lack of interest. Reduced participation in school events such as PTO/PTA held little relation to the strong academic support felt by the participants for academic objectives. By encouraging parental participation and by providing opportunities for meaningful family involvement, schools play a critical role in bridging the gulf between home and school. Both children and schools benefit when teachers and educational leaders use their knowledge about children's families and experiences outside the classroom to create individually and culturally relevant learning experiences.

Teachers and administrators who were lacking in cultural knowledge prompted the parents in my study to build strong community networks or to use strategies in an attempt to hold the schools accountable for their children's education. These two important tactics were major factors in the eventual academic success of the students involved in my study. These were useful for overcoming the mismatch between the teacher/student expectations and the teacher/parent school communication breakdowns parents encountered.

Role modeling and protecting their children's self esteem increased the parents' confidence for achieving positive educational outcomes although it was concluded that parents should focus on the present and not the past. The parents of successful students taught their children values and how to successfully respond when their own cultural values conflicted with mainstream expectations. They felt that they needed to fight for their children's rights. Family and home environments conducive to learning were essential for all the parents. This included providing resources and monitoring their children's assignments. In addition, they focused on getting their child's attention and keeping them focused.

Lisa Delpit (1995), a world-renowned researcher and author, studied how parenting styles influence the way cultures decode information/directives given to them at school. Her research revealed that certain groups of parents give clear directives containing no choices in their statements. For example, the statement "Go take your bath" contains no choices. One the other hand, "Don't you think it's time to take your bath?" contains a choice. Teachers, often use indirect statements such as, "I think it's time to move to the next activity," which results in students mistakenly perceiving a choice being offered. However, if the wrong choice is made, a discipline referral can be the result. Culturally inappropriate directives and questioning techniques used by a teacher may contribute to the disproportionate number of discipline referrals certain groups of children receive in school districts across the country. To improve student-teacher interactions, teachers may need better cultural training to support additional teaching pedagogies. In-service training on the appropriate use of questioning and directives could help teachers increase their effectiveness in facilitating improved student interactions so that students reach their full academic potential. Culture therapy would be an excellent way to bring self-awareness to educators, who are responsible for providing instruction to youth.

Philosophical differences between parents and school personnel regarding educational practices can present challenges to effective collaboration. Parent groups differ in their views of what constitutes desirable behavior on the part of their children. Moreover, they differ in their conceptions of the attributes that define optimal cultural development. Differences were evidenced in this study in the comments and strategies employed by the parents. Because of the identified differences, teachers' and administrators' perceptions of parental input may need to undergo major changes. Perceptions of the parental role should evolve from that of parents being viewed as a problem, or of individuals in need of *parent training* to enable them to comply with current institutional models and system rules, to a perception of parents as educational advocates, decision makers and valued school partners. This transformation must happen if schools want to receive parental support and want to involve the community in a way that places the family squarely in the center of the educational process.

Some parents expressed concerns that the school officials did not understand their culture. Their comments serve as a strong indicator of the need for culturally sensitive changes. Some of the parents, as a result of cultural barriers, have become dependent on social networks to help them navigate school-related issues. Cultural therapy should be implemented in the school to increase self-awareness among school officials.

To initiate the change process that is needed, universities and educational programs could investigate incorporating cultural therapy into their programs to increase awareness of cultural differences. This would serve to better equip future educators with the skills required for improving cultural relations. Teacher and administrator college preparation courses currently contain few mechanisms that demonstrate the inclusion of parents in schools' formal decision-making programs. The Harvard Family Research Project (1994) surveyed state certification requirements and preservice education programs to document the content of parent involvement requirements and training opportunities for Pre-K thru 12 teachers. They found that the majority of states do not mention parent involvement in their teacher or administrator certification requirements. When these types of programs do exist, the training they contain is often minimal and rather traditional.

Clearly, developing partnerships with families is complex and challenging. Parent-school partnerships do not mean that education professionals should abdicate their professional role. Instead, parents should be viewed as experts about their own particular cultural environment. The dilemma, of course, is how to value and include multiple perspectives, while at the same time advocating for educational practices that are based on the best understandings about how children develop and learn.

Through my experiences as a parent, my work as an educator of over 20 years, and my studies of effective parenting models and strategies, I sincerely desire to impact and reach as many families as possible in developing emotionally, physically, socially, and academically healthy children. All parents, irrespective of socio-economic status, race/ethnicity, or social standing *need help,* and schools and communities must work to provide support. When all stakeholders work cooperatively, our children reap the benefits.

References

Carnegie Task Force (1994). *Starting points: meeting the needs of our youngest children.*
URL: http://www.carnegie.org/startingpoints.

Charles, T., & O'Quinn, S. (2001). *Eliminating the Black-White achievement gap: A summary of research.* Chapel Hill: North Carolina Education Research Council.

Crnic, K & Lamberty, G. (1994). Reconsidering school readiness: conceptual and applied perspectives. *Early Education and Development, 5,* 91-105.

Erath, S., Flanagan, K., & Bierman, K. (2007). Social Anxiety and Peer Relations in Early Adolescence: Behavioral and Cognitive Factors. *Journal of Abnormal Child Psychology, 35,* 405-16. (Document ID: 1275906131). Retrieved September 20, 2008, from Research Library database.).

*Fleming, G. (2010). 10 Common test mistakes. Retrieved March 30, 2011 from http://homeworktips.about.com/od/schooltests/a/testmistakes.htm.

Delgado, R., & Stefancic, J. (2001) <u>Critical Race Theory</u>. New York: New York University Press.

Delpit, L. (1995) *Other People's Children: Cultural Conflict in the Classroom.* New York: The New Press.

Epstein, J. L. & Sanders, M. G. (2006). Creating Home-School Partnerships by Engaging Families in Schoolwide Positive Behavior Supports, Harvard Family Research Project. *Preparing teachers to* involve parents. *A national survey of teacher education programs.* Cambridge, MA.

Henderson, A., & Mapp, K. (2002). *A new wave of evidence: The impact of school, family, and community connections on student achievement.* Austin, TX: Southwest Educational Development Laboratory.

Learning First Alliance (2010). Safe and supportive schools. Washington, DC: Learning First Alliance.

McLellan, D.E. & Katz, L.G. (2001). *Assessing Young Children's Competence.* URL: http://ericeece.org.

McLeod, K. (2009). *Facilitator's Guide: Training Manual: Creating Cultural Responsiveness.* Creative Energy LLC

Muscott, H., Szczesiul, S., Berk, B., Staub, K., Hoover, J., & Perry-Chisholm, P. (2008). Creating Home-School Partnerships by Engaging Families in School wide Positive Behavior Supports. *Teaching Exceptional Children, 40,* 7-14. Retrieved August 4, 2008, from ProQuest Education Journals database.

National Association for the Education of Young Children. (1997). Early years are learning years. Retrieved March 30, 2011 from http://readyweb.crc.uiuc.edu/virtual-library/1997/learnabo.html.

National Association of State Mental Health Program Directors, and the National Association of State Directors of Special Education. (2002). Mental health, schools, and families working together for all children and youth: A shared agenda. Alexandria, VA: Author.

Ogbu, J. (2003). *Black American Students in an Affluent Suburb.* Portland, OR: Book News, Inc.

Ogbu, J. & H. Simon (1998). Voluntary and Involuntary Minorities: A

Cultural-Ecological Theory of School Performance with Some Implications for Education. *Anthropology and Education Quarterly 29:* 155-188.

Parker, J. G., Rubin, K. H., Erath, S. A., Wojslawowicz, J. C., & Buskirk, A. A. (2006). Peer relationships, child development, and adjustment: A developmental psychopathology perspective. In D. Cicchetti & D. J. Cohen (Eds.), *Developmental Psychopathology: Theory and Methods* (2nd Ed., Vol. 1, pp. 96-161). New York: Wiley.

Rumberger, R. W., & Larson, K. A. (1998). *Student mobility and the increased risk of high school dropout.* American Journal of Education, 107(1), 1-35.

Snow, K. L. (2006). Measuring School Readiness: Conceptual and Practical Considerations. *Early Education and Development, 17,* 17-41.

Sassu, R. (2007). The evaluation of school readiness for 5-8 years old children – cognitive, social-emotional, and motor coordination and physical health perspectives. *Cognitie, Creier, Comportament/Cognition, Brain, Behavior, 11,* 67-81. Retrieved September 20, 2008, from ProQuest Psychology Journals database.

Appendices

Resources for Parents and Schools

Appendix A – Summary of Parenting Strategies

Appendix B - Parent Positive Reinforcement Form

Appendix C - Co-Parenting Agenda Meeting Form

Appendix D - Home Rules Contract

Appendix A – Summary of Parenting Strategies

Table 1: Summary of Parenting Strategies

1. Encourage academic excellence early in life.
2. Provide each child with a designated study space.
3. Teach your child mainstream expectations and values to aid in their ability to successfully respond when those expectations conflict with personal and cultural values.
4. Reduce the number of hours spent watching television.
5. Link career aspirations to required academic efforts (i.e. to be a lawyer you need to become an avid reader).
6. Reduce time spent completing chores during the school week.
7. Strongly consider the rating of the school before moving.
8. Provide a conducive home environment for academic excellence that may include resources such as tutors, interactive videos, and books.
9. Provide each child with a library card.
10. Share financial correlation between degree of education and salary.
11. Role-Model expectations. For example, parents should go to the library and read with their children as early as

possible.
12. Join book clubs with child.
13. Monitor time away from home (K-12).
14. Closely monitor their children's associates. Make it a requirement to meet each associate.
15. Praise your child consistently for making good grades.
16. Encourage children to overcome barriers experienced at school by assuring the child that the school system has each child's best interest in mind.
17. Focus more energy on future goals. Do not allow the negative past to hinder your success.
18. Teach your children that education is the key to social mobility.
19. Surround your children with positive family members and mentors that have a strong value for education.
20. Verify school policy with outside sources in order to effectively communicate with school officials.
21. Have face-to-face conferences with school officials early in the school year to show that you care about your child's education.
22. Take responsibility for motivating and establishing a high value for education.
23. Communicate with school officials via email, notes, and conferences.
24. Increase your child's self-esteem by teaching the positive

	contributions of their ethnicity.
25.	Establish clear expectations. Re-enforce those expectations through discipline.

Appendix B – Positive Reinforcement Form

Name_____

Today, I learned a more respectful and responsible way to behave. Below is a picture of me doing it right.

[ ]

Date: _____
Note: Have your child explain the picture and/or the appropriate behavior.

Appendix C – Co-Parenting Agenda Meeting Form

1. Schedules: (ask: are there any changes or out of town appointments)

_____
_____

2. Academic Progress of child or children:

_____
_____

3. Behavioral Progress of child or children:

_____
_____

4. Issues or Concerns:

_____
_____

5. Agreements:

_____
_____

6. Agenda items to be discussed during the next meeting:

_____
_____

7. Summary:

_____
_____

Appendix D – Home Rules Contract

For the _____ **Family** (last name[s] of family).

All family members, whose signatures are present on this document, are in agreement with and will follow the rules and consequences of this Home Rules Contract as listed below:

1. Rule #1: (Write the rule below.)

_____

    Consequence:_____

    Privilege:_____

_____

2. Rule # 2: (Write the rule below.)

_____

    Consequence:_____

    Privilege:_____

_____

3. Rule # 3: (Write the rule below.)

_____

    Consequence:_____

    Privilege:_____

_____

4. Rule # 4: (Write the rule below.)

Consequence:_____

Privilege:_____

5. Rule # 5: (Write the rule below.)

Consequence:_____

Privilege:_____

Signatures of Family Members *(The contract must be signed by all family members involved in implementing the rules, consequences, and privileges. You can add additional members as necessary.)*

_____
Parent #1

_____
Parent #2

_____
Extended Family Member # 1

_____
Teenager #1

_____
Home Caregiver # 1

About the Author

Dr. Tyrone Tanner is a researcher and professor of education. He has 20 years of higher education and public school experience. He has held several education positions including working as a professor, a consultant (with expertise in parenting and assisting schools in increasing parent involvement), an urban school personnel director, and a middle and high school administrator and teacher.

Dr. Tanner's research has been published in more than 30 peer review journals and he has presented all over the United States and abroad. His research focuses on building effective parent/school relationships that increase parent involvement and provide educators with the tools needed to experience success with all students.

Dr. Tanner is also the founder of a non-profit organization, *CHILDREN'S BEST INTEREST*. His organization is working to secure the best interest of children by sharing co-parenting strategies for married or divorced couples, informing individuals of their attorney–client rights, and presenting a top notch parenting curriculum that focuses on assisting parents in developing the skills and strategies necessary to optimize their children's physical (health), intellectual (cognitive), psychological (self esteem), environmental (home conducive for learning), and social development - all of the areas needed to raise a healthy child.

While this book has been written from an academic viewpoint (best practices that are research based), Dr. Tanner has personally experienced the challenges of having a child with a partner with different parenting views, as well as experiencing the effects of divorce on a child and the aftermath of learning how to successfully move forward while focusing on the best interest of children. His groundbreaking research has touched the lives of thousands of families.

He received his Doctor of Education degree in Educational Leadership and Cultural Studies from the University of Houston, a Master of Education in School Administration and Supervision from Southern University, and a Bachelor of Arts in History Education from Newberry College.

Parents need Help TOO!

www.ingramcontent.com/pod-product-compliance
Lightning Source LLC
Chambersburg PA
CBHW071500160426
43195CB00013B/2166